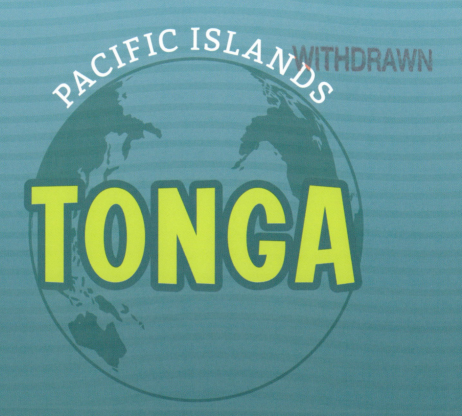

VOICES FROM AROUND THE WORLD

PACIFIC ISLANDS

WITHDRAWN

TONGA

Written by Dr. Ruth Toumu'a

with Tapukitea Lolomana'ia Rokolekutu

NORWOOD HOUSE PRESS

Norwood House Press

For more information about Norwood House Press please visit our website at www.norwoodhousepress.com or call 866-565-2900.

© 2023 Norwood House Press.

All rights reserved. No part of this book may be reproduced or utilized in any form or by any means without written permission from the publisher.

Credits

Editor: Mari Bolte
Designer: Sara Radka

Photo Credits

page 3: ©MikroArt / Shutterstock; page 4: ©mdurinik / Getty Images; page 4: ©Phil Walter / Staff / Getty Images; page 5: ©Dimitris66 / Getty Images; page 5: ©GEOATLAS - GRAPHI-OGRE / Shutterstock; page 6: ©OwenXie / Getty Images; page 7: ©Shyamal / Wikimedia; page 7: ©Nastasic / Getty Images; page 8: ©Nikhil Guhagarkar / Getty Images; page 9: ©FatSprat / Getty Images; page 10: ©Pnunn3 / Wikimedia; page 10: ©Dorling Kindersley / Getty Images; page 11: ©Rijksmuseum / lookandlearn.com; page 13: ©Dmitry Malov / Getty Images; page 14: ©Dolly MJ / Shutterstock; page 15: ©The New York Public Library / lookandlearn.com; page 15: ©Nastasic / Getty Images; page 16: ©REUTERS / Alamy; page 17: ©PawełMM / Wikimedia; page 19: ©mtcurado / Getty Images; page 20: ©maloff / Shutterstock; page 22: ©mtcurado / Getty Images; page 23: ©Fred Kruger/picture-alliance / DUMONT Bildar / Newscom; page 24: ©Tau'olunga / Wikimedia; page 25: ©Tim Graham/ robertharding / Newscom; page 26: ©James Strachan / Getty Images; page 27: ©Jeffrey Isaac Greenberg 10+ / Alamy; page 28: ©File Upload Bot (Magnus Manske) / Wikimedia; page 29: ©Cindy Miller Hopkins / Danita Delimont / Danita Delimont Photography / Newscom; page 31: ©Fred Kruger/picture-alliance / DUMONT Bildar / Newscom; page 32: ©Edwina Pickles/Fairfax Media / Stringer / Getty Images; page 33: ©Paskaran.T / Shutterstock; page 34: ©Danita Delimont Photography / Newscom; page 35: ©Kyodo / Newscom; page 36: ©Elmar Langle / Shutterstock; page 37: ©Mikko Laamanen / Getty Images; page 38: ©Danita Delimont / Shutterstock; page 39: ©Hel080808 / Dreamstime; page 40: ©bcampbell65 / Shutterstock; page 41: ©Steve Woods Photography / Getty Images; page 42: ©Fiona Goodall / Stringer / Getty Images; page 42: ©Oliver Strewe / Getty Images; page 43: ©daguimagery / Shutterstock; page 44: ©Rebecca Harding / Getty Images

Cover: ©maloff / Shutterstock; ©Susanne Michaela Huss / Getty Images

Library of Congress Cataloging-in-Publication Data

Names: Toumu'a, Ruth, 1977- author. | Rokolekutu, Tapukitea Lolomana'ia, consultant.
Title: Tonga / by Ruth Toumu'a ; consultant, Tapukitea Lolomana'ia Rokolekutu.
Description: [Chicago] : Norwood House Press, [2023] | Series: Voices from around the world : Pacific islands | Includes index. | Audience: Ages 8-10 | Audience: Grades 4-6 | Summary: "The islands of Tonga are full of rich history and culture. Describes the history, customs, geography, and culture of the people who live there, and provides authentic vocabulary words for an immersive experience. Includes a glossary, index, and bibliography for further reading"-- Provided by publisher.
Identifiers: LCCN 2022018962 (print) | LCCN 2022018963 (ebook) | ISBN 9781684507467 (hardcover) | ISBN 9781684048151 (paperback) | ISBN 9781684048205 (epub)
Subjects: LCSH: Tonga--Juvenile literature.
Classification: LCC DU880 .T68 2023 (print) | LCC DU880 (ebook) | DDC 996.12--dc23/eng/20220505
LC record available at https://lccn.loc.gov/2022018962
LC ebook record available at https://lccn.loc.gov/2022018963

Hardcover ISBN: 978-1-68450-746-7
Paperback ISBN: 978-1-68404-815-1

353N—082022
Manufactured in the United States of America in North Mankato, Minnesota.

Table of Contents

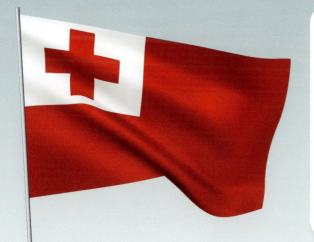

GUIDE TO PRONOUNCING
TONGAN VOWELS

A (like c<u>a</u>r)

E (like <u>e</u>gg)

I (like f<u>ee</u>t)

O (like <u>oar</u>)

U (like y<u>ou</u>)

Welcome to
Tonga

Mālō e lelei! This is how people greet each other in Tonga. It expresses thankfulness. People are thankful to be meeting with each other. They are thankful that they are well, and things are good.

Tongan is a Polynesian language.

Where is Tonga?

The Kingdom of Tonga is an **archipelago**. It is in the heart of the Pacific Ocean. There are more than 170 islands in Tonga. People live on about 36 of them. The islands of Tonga are a mixture of volcanic and coral islands. They are sorted into four main groups: Tongatapu, Ha'apai, Vava'u, and Niua.

Tongatapu is the main island, and Nuku'alofa is the country's capital.

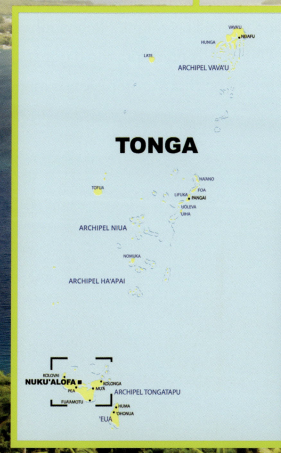

CHAPTER 1

The History of Tonga

On modern maps, the Tongan islands are just west of the international date line. That means Tonga is one of the first countries in the world to see each new day.

In Tongan legends, Maui was a powerful ancestor. He was visiting a place called Manuʻa in Sāmoa. An old chiefly man there gave him a very special fishing hook. While fishing, Maui felt his hook snag something. He tried to pull, but it was stuck. Maui pulled and pulled with all his might. He brought an island up from the bottom of the sea. This was Tongatapu, the biggest island in Tonga. On later fishing trips, he pulled up many other islands in Tonga, and some in Fiji and Sāmoa too.

The view from Mount Talau, on the main island of Vavaʻu, overlooks the rain forest.

Tonga has two seasons. The hot, humid season is from December to April. A cooler dry season lasts from May to November.

Many plants and animals call Tonga home. Some are found nowhere else on Earth. The Tongan megapode is one of these. It's a small bird that buries its eggs on the side of volcanoes. The warm soil there helps the eggs hatch.

Tongan megapode

Plant and animal life gave everything people needed in the past. For example, the coconut tree provided food for people and animals. It also gave shade, shelter, timber, rope, fiber, and fuel. Coconut oil was used for medicines and beauty products.

Coconut palms grow well throughout Tonga.

Husks are the dry outer covering of fruits and seeds, like coconuts.

Another important item made from the coconut tree is *kafa*, also called sennit. It is made with coconut husk fibers. For thousands of years, the fishing lines, ropes, and cords in Tonga were made from kafa.

Many cultures in the Pacific make and use kafa. In other Pacific languages, it is called *kaha, aha, ka'a, kawa, gaha,* or *kapa.*

DID YOU KNOW?

The husk of the *niu kafa* (wild coconut) is best for making kafa. It's more oval shaped than other coconuts. The fiber inside is longer and easier to make rope from.

It can take months to make kafa rope. It's hard work. First, the husks are pulled off the mature dry niu kafa. They are soaked in seawater for several weeks. Next, the soaked husks are beaten with a mallet. The long strands of fiber are pulled out. Then, they are rinsed and dried in the sun.

After that, the clean, dry fibers are **plaited**. This plaited rope is very strong and lasts a long time. It can stand up to salty seawater.

Kafa has been used for both everyday activities and special ceremonies. It is strong, lasts a long time, and is a locally grown renewable resource.

People have lived in the Tongan islands for about 3,000 years. The first people arrived from the western Pacific around 900 BCE. They are called "Lapita people." The name comes from the unique style of pottery they made and used. Lapita pottery was made from clay. It was decorated with geometric patterns made by pressing a stamp into the wet clay when the pot was formed. These Lapita people were the ancestors of Tongans and many other Pacific people today.

Nobody knows for sure why these people left their homeland and sailed into the unknown. Some ideas include overpopulation, **famine**, or war. Perhaps, it was about land. Maybe, as the population grew, the land was given to the older sons. The younger sons would have had to find new land for themselves.

Lapita pottery was used for cooking, serving, and storage.

Tongan kalia were made without nails or screws. Instead, complex woodwork and kafa bindings held the boat together.

Ancient Tongans had great boat-building technology and **navigation** skills. They used the stars, moon, sun, wind, and ocean currents to navigate. They were the first to sail deep into the huge, unmapped Pacific Ocean.

Some famous Tongan *kalia* (double-hulled canoes) could carry 100 or more people. Kafa ropes were vital for building and sailing these vessels. These amazing boats sailed the Pacific Ocean like a highway.

Hundreds of years later, European people followed. Dutch explorers Schouten and Le Maire found Tonga in 1616 and traded with locals. Abel Tasman visited in 1643 and British explorer Captain Cook in 1773, 1774, and 1777. Cook called Tonga the "Friendly Islands."

Tonga's society then was already well developed and stable. There were different social classes of people. The highest was the royal family. The *Tuʻi Tonga* (king), ruled all of Tonga. Chiefs were next. There were several kinds of chiefs with different roles in leading people and supporting the king. The chiefly title passed from father to son. Finally, the common people made up the rest of society.

People speak *Lea Faka-Tonga* (Tongan language) as their first language. There is also another native language, Niuafoʻou. It is spoken in the northern islands. Today, English is the most common second language.

To speak to each other, common people would use normal everyday Tongan words. But to speak politely to the chiefs, common people used different words. To speak to royalty, everyone used the language for the king. It has regal words instead of everyday words. These regal words were more poetic and sometimes had special meanings.

The history of the Tongan royal family dates back to around 950 CE. The first Tuʻi Tonga was Ahoʻeitu. Spoken history says he was the son of a sky god and a human mother. The Tuʻi Tonga in ancient times were very powerful. Some built amazing structures during their time as king.

The eleventh Tuʻi Tonga was Tuʻitātui. His royal **compound** was known as Heketā. It was built around 1200 CE. It stood on the Eastern side of Tongatapu. Today, there are still several remarkable monuments built during his reign. One is the stone trilithon called Haʻamonga a Maui (the burden of Maui).

The Haʻamonga a Maui stands on the island of Tongatapu.

Tonga's Stonehenge

The Haʻamonga a Maui trilithon is about 16.4 feet (5 meters) high and about 20 feet (6 m) long. It's built from three large slabs of limestone rock. The stones weigh more than 30 tons (27.2 metric tons). People believe it was a gateway and perhaps a monument to Tuʻitātuiʻs two sons. They are represented by the two upright stones. And they carry a shared burden. Some also believe it was an ancient calendar. In 1966, King Tāufaʻāhau Tupou IV discovered carved marks on the top that show where the sun rises at important times of the year.

In the past, people ate a very healthy diet. Seafood and birds were hunted. Root crops, breadfruit, tropical fruit, and coconut were gathered.

Food was baked in an 'umu (underground earth oven). It was also steamed in large pottery bowls or packages wrapped in banana leaves. Seafood was eaten fresh from the ocean.

Raw fish marinated in lemon and coconut cream is a popular dish.

People dressed in clothing made from *ngatu* (bark cloth) wrapped around their bodies. It was secured with *sisī lousi* (soft fiber rope) made from a long-leafed plant called *sī*.

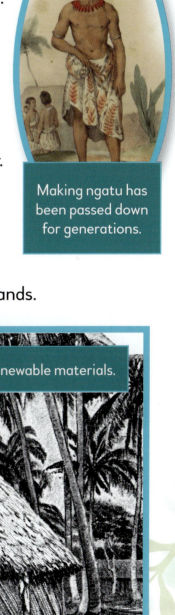

Traditionally, people in Tonga lived in *fale* (oval-shaped homes). Tongan fale had a strong timber structure. Walls were made from woven coconut leaves. The roof was thatched with coconut and other long leaves. Building the fale took a lot of skill and labor.

Making ngatu has been passed down for generations.

Fale were cool in the hot season. They held in the warmth in the cooler season. The unique roof shape could keep out heavy rain and strong winds. People still build fale today, especially in the more remote outer islands.

Fale were built with naturally occurring and renewable materials.

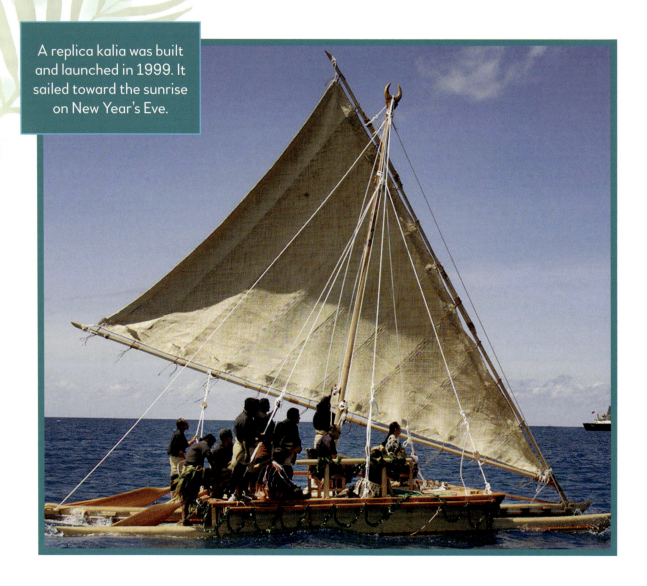

A replica kalia was built and launched in 1999. It sailed toward the sunrise on New Year's Eve.

Tonga's kalia, sailing skills, leadership, and stable society helped them to grow strong. From around 1200 to 1500, the Tu'i Tonga built a huge South Pacific **empire**. It included parts of Fiji and both the Sāmoan Islands. It also included the island nations of Niue, Rotuma, Tokelau, Futuna, and Uvea. Parts of the Solomon Islands were also included.

The Tuʻi Tonga's ocean army took control of islands. Governors were put in place as leaders. During this time, learning and borrowing occurred between the cultures of the empire. Sometimes, people on those islands intermarried.

Eventually, Sāmoa fought to be free from the empire again. Other islands became free too. After this, the empire moved back to control its own islands in Tonga.

After several hundred years of stable history, rivalries developed. From the end of the 1700s to the middle of the 1800s, Tonga experienced fighting and conflict. Some of the chiefs started to compete for power, land, and wealth. War weapons like wooden clubs were used for fighting. Sadly, many people died during the conflicts.

Eventually, though, the whole of Tonga was unified again in 1845. The country was under the rule of one leader, Tāufaʻāhau Tupou I.

Tāufaʻāhau Tupou I, also known as George Tupou I, reigned from 1845 to 1893.

CHAPTER 2

Island Traditions

Tonga has never been **colonized** by a foreign nation. This was mostly because of the political skills of Tonga's leaders and advisers at that time. In 1875, Tonga's **constitution** was written. In 1900, a Treaty of Friendship was signed with Great Britain.

Today, Tonga is a constitutional monarchy. It has a king or queen who act together with the **parliament**. Together, they govern the country.

Tonga is the last kingdom in the Pacific. It is an independent nation and is part of the United Nations. Thanks to the Treaty of Friendship with Great Britain, it is also part of the Commonwealth of Nations.

Traditionally, the king lived in specially built fale. But more than 150 years ago, a European-style wooden palace was built. It is on the waterfront in the center of the capital city, Nuku'alofa. When the king is there, the flag flies high from the rooftop. Tonga's parliament buildings are nearby.

The Royal Palace on Tongatapu is the official residence of the Tongan royal family. It was built in 1867. The royal coat of arms flies at the top.

Ta'ovala can be handed down from one generation to the next.

Tongan culture has grown core values over its 2,000-plus years of existence. These values affect how people think, act, and feel. Four values are very important.

The first says that every person deserves the right kind of respect. Sharing, working together, and doing right by each other is core to the second value. The third value says to be humble and never too proud to help others. The fourth requires keeping good and loyal relationships with others.

Tongan people wear a sign of respect called a *ta'ovala*. It is a special finely woven mat worn around the waist. It is usually made from pandanus leaves or hibiscus bark. It is held in place with a length of kafa.

Legend says that long ago, some sailors traveled to the Tu'i Tonga. They arrived in ragged clothing after a very rough sea trip. Out of respect, they cut down their valuable woven sail. They cut it into pieces to wrap around themselves. They wanted to be dressed well before seeing their king.

There are a number of different types of ta'ovala. Each is worn for different events and purposes. But everyone wears them.

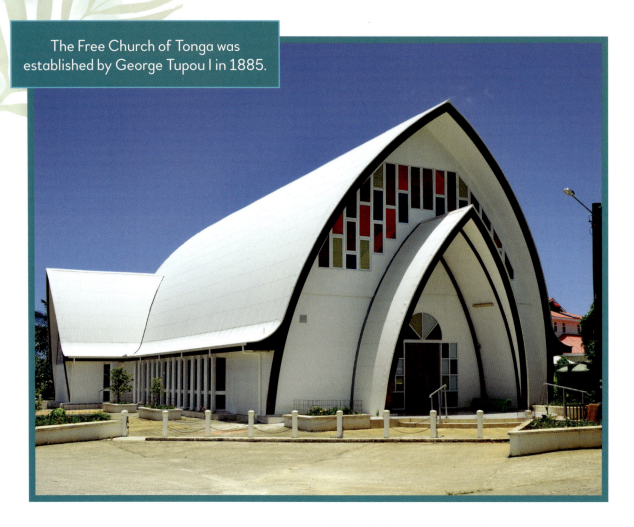

The Free Church of Tonga was established by George Tupou I in 1885.

British missionaries arrived in the late 1700s. Since then, Christian religion has been strongly observed in Tonga. King Tupou I dedicated Tonga to the Christian God.

Religion shapes many things about life in Tonga today. People are encouraged to dress conservatively and modestly. Businesses are not open on Sunday, to allow people a day of rest. There are no flights out of the airport on that day.

Each village has a number of church buildings. The sound of church bells fills the air each Sunday.

Another historical event that shaped Tonga is Emancipation Day. It is an annual public holiday. In 1862, King George Tupou I declared liberty for all. This is viewed as a turning point in Tonga's history. From that day, common people could live without the fear of being forced to work for the chiefs. They were given land of their own to live on and grow food.

The St. Antonius Basilica Church has a distinctive cone-shaped roof.

In ancient Tonga, there were several important events that happened each year. There were times when gifts were given to the Tu'i Tonga. Gifts included the first fruits of the harvest. This was important for confirming and strengthening ties to the king. This is still done today. Villages and their talking chiefs will visit the palace. Goods are presented, and connections with the royal family are confirmed.

In modern Tonga, families also celebrate holidays like Christmas, Easter, and New Year's. Children's Sunday, Mother's Day, and Father's Day are also holidays. First birthdays, 21st birthdays, weddings, and graduations are all important celebrations.

In July, there is a special weeklong celebration. It is called the Tonga Heilala Festival. *Heilala* is Tonga's national flower. The festival includes the king's birthday celebrations on July 4. There are street float parades, traditional and modern musical events, and competitions. There is also a beauty pageant, balls, and lots of food.

heilala flower

Celebration Feasts

Kai pola (feasts) are the traditional way that many important events were celebrated. The foods have changed a bit over time, and so have the utensils. Plates and cutlery have replaced banana leaves and fingers. Some international dishes like potato salad have been adapted to local tastes and added to traditional foods at the kai pola. Instead of green coconuts to drink, some people now serve small bottles of soda. The food may change, but the important role in showing love, happiness, and generosity stays the same.

CHAPTER 3

Tonga Today

Modern life in Tonga has brought changes. But there are still many traditional activities. They are as important today as they were hundreds of years ago.

Some fine goods are handmade by women. They include ngatu, woven items like ta'ovala, and other ceremonial mats. Sometimes they include decorated kafa too. They are given at special events.

These items are often family heirlooms. They are exchanged at weddings and funerals. This tradition keeps the community together. The women in Tonga know when and how to exchange these important pieces.

Ngatu is a fabric made from the bark of the paper mulberry tree. Designs are painted onto the fabric.

Making and giving floral or shell necklaces is an important custom. It takes skill, knowledge, and time to make them. They are made for guests of honor at important events.

Making them starts with picking and choosing only the best flowers and leaves. Next, the parts are sewn or woven together. Finally, it is gifted to the special person.

The flower garland is a sign of love and respect for the person who wears it. Each flower has a special meaning in the Tongan way of life.

Floral necklaces are personal gifts that signify relationships between people in the community.

All cultures change over time. Today's Tonga is no exception. A couple of decades ago, people always chose formal Tongan outfits to go to the capital, Nuku'alofa. Women always wore skirts and dresses in public. Today, most people wear casual clothing. Some women dress in pants, jeans, and shorts.

On the rural roads 20 years ago, families used horse-drawn carts to travel. Today, vehicles fill the roads.

DID YOU KNOW?

There are no traffic lights on Tonga.
Roundabouts are used to help the flow of traffic.

Nuku'alofa is Tonga's largest city.

Garbage disposal and recycling are big challenges in small island countries like Tonga. Everything that isn't consumed stays on the island and has to be disposed of as garbage.

Tonga's economy used to rely on dried coconut flesh that is used to make coconut oil. But it is no longer processed to be sold overseas. Tonga's modern economy still relies on agriculture, though. Crops like squash, pumpkin, watermelon, and vanilla are grown for overseas markets. Root crops like taro, cassava, yams, and sweet potatoes are also exported.

Sweet potatoes, giant taro, and taro at a Tongan market.

As lifestyles, diets, and beliefs change, some traditions are lost. For example, sharks were an important part of religion and culture in ancient Tongan times. Lassoing sharks was once practiced by people from certain islands.

The brave crew acted in harmony during the trip. Traditional rattles and bait were used to attract sharks. The lead fisherman said special words. The crew gave the first captured shark a gift of flowers and the dried, powdered roots of the *kava* plant.

The fishing crew excited the sharks by beating the water. Then, they lassoed the sharks using kafa ropes. They took the caught sharks back to the village. The people sang to the fishermen in appreciation.

Kafa was used for more than fishing. In ancient Tonga, the posts of the king's fale were bound together using kafa. There was no need for nails. Tying, or lashing, in geometric patterns to decorate the royal buildings is called *lalava*. Lalava adds strength and beauty to the building. This art form is not common today.

Today, few people have the skills or the time to make traditional kafa. Instead, synthetic fibers like wool or nylon are used. Nowadays, kafa is almost only used for tying ta'ovala.

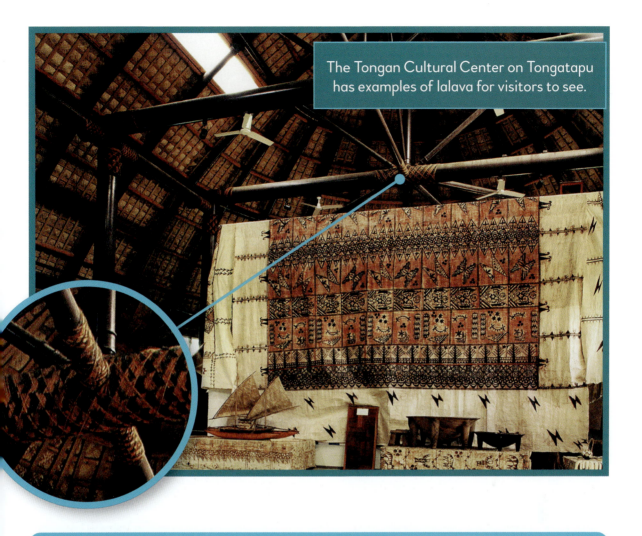

The Tongan Cultural Center on Tongatapu has examples of lalava for visitors to see.

Lalava Art

Lalava designs and symbols all have special meanings in Tongan culture. The master of lalava, Tamale of Niutoua, decides on the patterns. His young helpers wind the black-, brown-, or tan-colored kafa around and around the beams in a fale to create these designs. Some designs are also seen in other Tongan art forms such as ngatu, *fala* (mat) weaving, and *ta tatau* (tattoos).

Schoolchildren dressed in traditional clothing for the coronation of King Tupou VI in 2015.

For Tongan people, family has a broad meaning. A family might include adopted children, cousins, grandparents, aunts, and uncles all living together. A person may not have much money, but they are never poor if they have family.

As a child grows up, they learn who everyone is and how they are related to them. They learn about past generations too. These lessons are remembered for their whole lives. As they grow, they should act in ways that honor these family ties.

Families may disagree, but they stick together. That's what gets people through all kinds of challenges in life. The whole family celebrates one member's achievement or good fortune.

Over the years, Tongan people have moved to other countries around the world. Many live in New Zealand, Australia, the United Kingdom, and the United States. Even when Tongan people move overseas, they usually keep family ties strong.

Tongan people around the world celebrate their heritage.

Growing up in Tonga today is different from the past. More families have moved to town areas for work and school. But most families will still have a piece of family land. Here, they grow the root crops, fruit, and vegetables. They may grow them for personal use or sell them. Most boys learn how to farm or fish. Most girls will help take care of their home and siblings.

DID YOU KNOW?

Nature is still a big part of island life. Homes often have animals in the yard around them.

Pigs, chickens, and dogs are common yard animals.

Primary schools are free for children to attend.

Church activities like Sunday school and choir practice are done on the weekend. Nearly all children go to a local primary school. Schools are run by the government or a church. Children read and write in the Tongan language and learn Tongan culture and arts. Other school subjects are studied too. English is slowly introduced. By the end of secondary school, most learning is in English.

Children still have a lot of freedom to safely roam and play. They explore the village and surrounding area. There will always be someone watching out for them.

In the past, children made kites, skipped, and raced. They played marbles, rode horses, and caught crabs. But now, more kids have access to technology. It's changing how they play.

Radio and television have helped Tongans communicate for decades. In 2013, broadband internet was provided for the first time. Undersea cables stretch along the ocean floor from a landing station in Fiji. Computers and the internet are still expensive. Not everyone has them. But they are getting more and more common.

Computers are used for most office work. Other modern technology is used in health care, business, and farming. Some homes on the outer islands use solar power. Tonga is investing in solar and wind power. The country aims to be using 70 percent renewable energy by 2030.

Renewable energy comes from a source that is not depleted when it is used. Tonga has plenty of sun and wind to supply its needs.

Uolova looks uninhabited, but many people visit the island for its beauty and remoteness.

There are still many places in Tonga that look and feel untouched. Many small and beautiful islands have no one living on them. They are often still in their natural state.

Tonga has land and marine nature reserves, national parks, and sanctuaries. On 'Eua island, the rainforest in the national park is much like it was thousands of years ago. There is a tree there that is over 800 years old.

Tonga's Haʻapai Islands are known for turquoise waters and beautiful beaches.

Tonga is a great destination for tourists. They visit white sand beaches, cliffs, and volcanoes. Forests and coral reefs can be explored.

Niuafo'ou is a volcanic ring island with a lagoon in the center. The Vava'u islands are mountainous. They are a beautiful place to see while sailing. The Ha'apai island group lets visitors experience traditional small island life. Tongatapu has many important historical sites and lots of cultural entertainment.

Tonga's music, food, dance, and art all provide rich experiences. Tourists can watch or join in making handicrafts. They can attend a kava ceremony. Hearing Tongan people harmonize in church is a special sound.

Kava is used in ceremonies and as a relaxing drink. It is prepared in a large carved wooden bowl with three or more legs.

Tonga is full of opportunities for underwater adventures.

People who like outdoor activities can go hiking, camping, and horse riding. They can try scuba diving, snorkeling, surfing, fishing, and kayaking. The slow pace of life and nice climate is relaxing.

Whale watching has become an important tourist activity in the past decade. In June and July, whales can be seen from beaches. Tour companies take people out on boats to see the whales up close.

Whales and Warm Water

During the winter months, the waters down south in the Antarctic Ocean are too cold. So, whales migrate to Tongan waters where the sea is warmer. They breed and raise their young there for a couple of months. Because of strong conservation efforts over the past couple of decades, the population of humpback whales has grown. But they still need to be protected.

The Tongan national rugby league team always starts games with a war dance called the Sipi Tau.

People love living in Tonga. They like to laugh and tell a good joke. And they are passionate about supporting their rugby teams.

Because it is a small country, people know each other. In a village, lots of people are related. This gives everyone a strong sense of belonging and being connected. In Tonga, it is possible to live simply and be happy.

Families and friends are close in Tonga.

Tongan history and culture is very rich and meaningful. It's central to people's lives. Because of this, it is important to respect local customs when visiting. It is also important for Tongan people to preserve the special aspects of their culture and language.

Small outrigger canoes are still sometimes used in Tonga today.

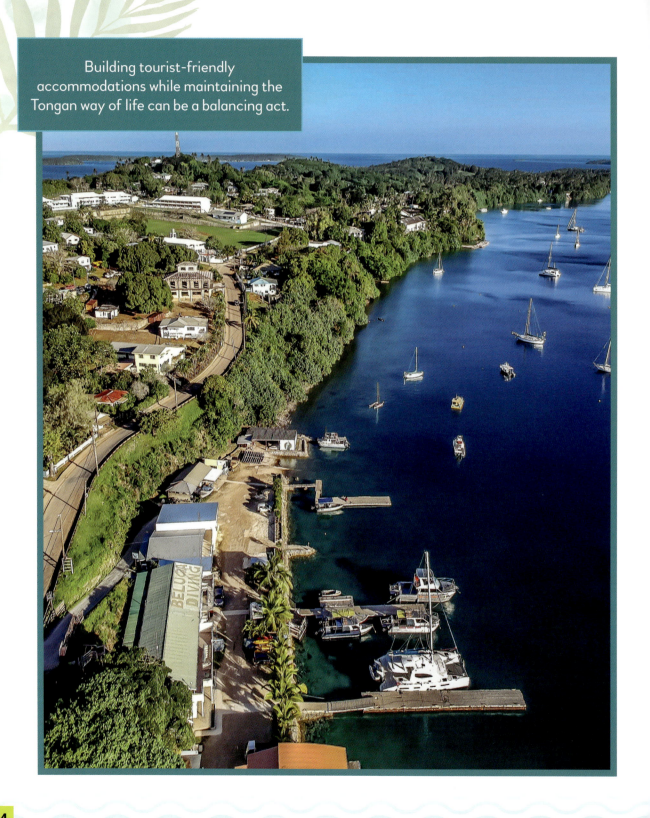

Building tourist-friendly accommodations while maintaining the Tongan way of life can be a balancing act.

Tonga is embracing new things that development and technology can bring. Computers are used for most office work, and modern technology is used in health care, business, and farming. Modern technology makes many of these processes more efficient.

Responsible tourism means caring for the island and the people who live there.

At the same time, it's important to try to minimize the negative effects that some of these things can have. But sometimes, we don't know the negative effects until much later on.

Like all South Pacific nations, Tonga's challenge is to find a healthy balance between the old and the new. The strands of modern and traditional life must be carefully plaited together like kafa.

Tongan Glossary

Remember to check page 3 for tips on pronunciation!

fala: traditional Tongan mat woven from dried pandanus leaves

fale: traditional Tongan-style house or building

heilala: a flower used to make the garland of the king and chiefs

kafa: sennit rope made from coconut fibers

kai pola: a traditional Tongan feast where special foods were placed on fresh woven green coconut mats and invited guests were seated around them to eat

kalia: double-hulled canoes

kava: a type of plant from the pepper family

lalava: ornamental lashing of the beams and poles of a fale with kafa rope

Lea Faka-Tonga: the Tongan language

mālō e lelei: Tongan greeting

ngatu: bark cloth made from mulberry bark

niu kafa: a type of wild coconut tree bearing coconuts that are longer and more oval shaped than other types of coconut

sī: cordyline plant

sisī lousi: soft fiber rope

ta'ovala: a woven mat worn around the waist

ta tatau: traditional tattoos

Tu'i Tonga: king of Tonga

'umu: underground earth oven

English Glossary

archipelago (ahr-kuh-PEL-uh-go): an island, or group of islands

colonized (KAH-luh-nyzd): to be claimed or established by a group of settlers

compound (KOM-pownd): a cluster of buildings

constitution (KAHN-stuh-too-shuhn): basic laws of a nation, state, or group

empire (EM-py-uhr): a group of states or countries ruled by a single individual

famine (FAM-uhn): extreme scarcity of food

navigation (nav-uh-GAY-shuhn): monitoring and controlling the movement of a craft or vehicle from one place to another

parliament (PAR-luh-mehnt): a legislative body of government

plaited (PLAY-tuhd): braided

Read More about the Pacific Islands

Books

Spanier, Kristine. *New Zealand*. Minneapolis, MN: Jump!, Inc., 2022.

Vunidilo, Tarisi. *Fiji*. Chicago, IL: Norwood House Press, 2023.

Websites

Fun Facts about Tonga for Kids (https://tongapocketguide.com/fun-facts-about-tonga-for-kids/) Learn fun facts about the islands.

Tonga Holiday (http://www.tongaholiday.com/) Find out fun things to do in Tonga.

Index

About the Author

Dr. Ruth Toumu'a has lived and worked in Tonga since 1990. She studied Applied Linguistics and Education and has worked as a high school and university educator for over 20 years. She lives in New Zealand and for the last decade has been involved in publishing books that champion Pacific languages and cultures.

About the Consultant

Tapukitea L. Rokolekutu is a teacher by profession. She taught high school in Tonga for 10 years and history/politics and sociology at RMI-USP Campus, Majuro, Marshall Islands for 14. She also worked for the government of Tonga in the Prime Minister's Office and the Central Planning Office. She plans on returning to Tonga after completing her three-year contract at the USP Campus in the Marshall Islands. There, she will help the local community by teaching those in need.